W9-AKY-544

Getting to Know

Yellowstone National Park

by Patty Knapp

CHILDREN'S OUTDOOR LIBRARY
MOOSE, WYOMING

To Kandy, Caileen, and Justin

Copyright © 1997 by M.I. Adventure Publications. All rights reserved. No part of this book may be reproduced in any way, or by any means, without written permission except for in the case of brief quotations in a review.

Children's Outdoor Library, M.I. Adventure Publications,
P.O. Box 277, Moose, WY 83012

Art: "Fact or Fiction" cartoons (pg. 6, 8,10,12,18,19, 20, 22, 26, 30, 31, 34, 37) — Jackie Czapla
Above: Bison herd in front of Cutoff Mountain   JEFF & ALEXA HENRY
Front Cover: Grand Canyon of the Yellowstone   PATTY FURBUSH
Back Cover: Grizzly bear cub   MICHAEL H. FRANCIS
Poster: Grand Geyser   PATTY FURBUSH

Designed and published in the U.S.A.
Printed in Hong Kong

ISBN 0-9616395-8-X (softcover), 0-9616395-9-8 (hardcover)
Library of Congress Catalog Card Number: 97-65073

TABLE OF CONTENTS

Acknowledgements

Thanks to members of Yellowstone and Grand Teton National Park staff; students and teachers of S.A.D. 60, Maine; Kelly, Wyoming; and Yellowstone elementary schools; and helpful friends and family. Special thanks to park staff — Ellen Petrick-Underwood, Jim Peacos, Morgan Miller, Ann Deutch, Linda Jeske, Bill Wise, Jennifer Whipple; Ms. Carol Marcotte and her 3rd Grade class —Ashley, Amanda A., Amanda W., Allan, Sarah, Ryan D. Ryan L., Marie, Nick, Lauren, Daphne, Scott, Sasha, Joe, Jeremy, Lena; Mr. Dan Thomasma and his 4/5 grade class — Chester, Garrett, Chris, Deon, Sharon, Melissa, Chapelle, Aaron, Jason, and Carolyn; Ms. Barbara Rodden and her 7th grade class — Cody, Trisha, Sarah, Brian, Jerad, Ashley, David, Steve, Billy, Joslyn, Amanda, Katie, Sarah, Sonia, Justin; Ms. Cathy Maxam and 4th grade students Johnathan and Jennifer; Mrs. Tana Scholly and her 4th and 6th grade students— Kelly, Lindsay, Danny, Joshua, Laura, Jeremy, Ethan; Mrs. Kathleen King and her 6th grade students — Danielle, Kristie, Ian, Russell, Nick, Candice; Ms. Donna Barnes and her 5th grade class — Eliza, Garret, Britany, Steven, Holly, Kevin, Curtis, Jeremy, Monique, Kristin, Josh, Lee, Beth, Samantha, Christa, Ashley, Vernon, Mallory; Mr. Bill Fulford and son Will; and friends and family — Peggy Furbush, Caileen Nutter, Kip Knapp, Mary Nutter, and Justin King.

JEFF AND ALEXA HENRY

Old Faithful Geyser (receding eruption) and Old Faithful Inn

WELCOME TO YELLOWSTONE NATIONAL PARK

"MI-TSI-A-DA-ZI." That's the Minnetaree Sioux (*su*) name for Yellowstone. It means rock yellow water. In English, we would say yellow rock and water. That's what the Indians saw at Yellowstone in the 1800's and before. And that's what you will see when you travel through Yellowstone National Park.

Yellowstone is a world of wonder made spectacular by water, rock, and yellow colors. Water and *magma* (hot liquid rock) create the fascinating *thermal features*. Beautiful yellow colors surround many of these features.

It's yellow rock and water that create the beauty of Grand Canyon of the Yellowstone. There you will find a swift river and thundering waterfalls carving through a deep canyon. Shades of yellow tint the sculptured cliffs.

Say "Mi-tsi-a-da-zi" or "Yellowstone". What do you think of? Do you think of geysers, perhaps Old Faithful? Do you think of wildlife — bison and elk herds? Do you think, "It's the world's first national park!"?

Yellowstone is famous for many reasons including all the reasons just stated. This book will help you explore Yellowstone and learn its secrets. You'll have fun as you discover and learn about the park.

You can record your discoveries in the nature log at the back of the book. Use the map on pages 46 and 47 to help guide you on your adventure. The orange numbered circles found throughout the book refer to the locations marked on this map.

You'll find several green text boxes throughout the book. Read the first statement of each box and decide if it is fact or fiction. Then read the remaining paragraphs in the box. You might change your answer after reading the whole box. Keep track of how many "Fact or Fiction" questions you get right on your first guess. Compare your results to the Explorer Thermometer on the answer page.

Are you ready? Go explore and have fun.

OLD FAITHFUL—KING OF GEYSERS

Everyone who visits Yellowstone must see Old Faithful **15**. It is the "World's Most Famous Geyser." In a park with over two hundred geysers, why is Old Faithful so special? It isn't the largest or highest *geyser*. It's not the most frequent nor the most consistent geyser. It is, however, the most frequent **and** consistent of the **large** geysers.

Since its discovery, Old Faithful has changed little. Its height (100 -180'), eruption duration (1.5 - 5 minutes), and time between eruptions (about 75 minutes) has remained about the same. It is as dependable today as when the park was created.

Rangers use a formula to predict the eruptions. The prediction depends upon the time and duration of the previous eruption. Ask for the formula at the visitor center. Watch Old Faithful and see if you can predict the next eruption.

Some of Yellowstone's other geysers are pictured on the following pages. Read about them. On your travels through Yellowstone,

Old Faithful

visit some of these geysers. Although not as famous as Old Faithful, each geyser is spectacular. Check a visitor center for eruption times.

FACT OR FICTION:

The National Park Service built Yellowstone's boardwalks to make it easy to walk through *thermal* areas.

Thermal basins have a thin, delicate crust of soil and *minerals*. Walking on thermal areas damages the features. The edges of some features could collapse. Boiling water might be under the thin crust.

People have been burned or killed when they got off trails in thermal areas. For the protection of you and the thermal basins, PLEASE STAY ON THE BOARDWALKS. (Now you know the statement is fiction.)

PHOTOS BY PATTY FURBUSH

👆 Grotto geyser has an unusual shaped cone. Experts think the cone's shape is the result of geyserite covering tree trunks. Grotto geyser erupts to about ten feet. Erupting water splashes against the irregular cone and gives this geyser a unique appearance. Look for Grotto in Upper Geyser Basin ⑮.

NATIONAL PARK SERVICE

👆 Castle Geyser might be the oldest geyser in the park. It has the largest geyser cone in Yellowstone. This beautiful and powerful geyser only erupts every 10-12 hours. Powerful spurts of water erupt up to 90 feet. When the water falls, it cascades down the irregular shaped cone. Following the eruption, there is roaring steam phase of 30-40 minutes. Look for Castle Geyser in Upper Geyser Basin ⑮.

👉 Steamboat Geyser is the world's tallest active geyser. It has erupted up to 400 feet high (height of a 40 story building).

Unfortunately, its major eruptions are unpredictable and infrequent. Steamboat often spouts small columns of water and steam. However, its last major eruption was in 1991. Look for Steamboat Geyser in Norris Geyser Basin ㉒.

FACT OR FICTION:

Old Faithful is the tallest, predictable geyser in the world.

Old Faithful's eruptions can reach up to 180 feet high. Grand Geyser erupts up to 200 feet high. It is the tallest predictable geyser in the world. Grand erupts with 1-4 powerful bursts every 7-15 hours.

Old Faithful is more famous than Grand (on the poster) because it erupts more frequently. (Now you know the statement is fiction.)

☞ White Dome Geyser has a massive cone. It looks like a large geyser. However, eruptions only reach up to 30' in height. The cone's size and frequency of eruptions (sometimes every 15 minutes) make this an exciting geyser. Look for White Dome Geyser along Firehole Lake Drive ⑲.

🖐 Echinus ($\bar{e}$-$k\bar{i}$'-*nus*) Geyser's eruptions can easily be predicted. It has a large open crater that gradually fills with water. When the water reaches a certain level, steam and water erupt 40-60' high. The eruptions may last up to 60 minutes. After the eruption, water quickly drains down the vent. Look for Echinus in Norris Geyser Basin ㉑.

☞ One of Yellowstone's most picturesque geysers is Riverside Geyser. This geyser's eruptions arch over the Firehole River. Look for water running over the edge of the geyser cone. It signals an eruption within the next two hours. The eruptions occur about every 6-7 hours. Look for Riverside in the Upper Geyser Basin ⑮.

HOT SPRING OR GEYSER

There are over 10,000 *thermal features* in Yellowstone National Park. Thermal means that heat creates the features. About 200-250 of these features are geysers. Yellowstone has more geysers and other thermal features than the rest of the world combined.

All thermal features need three ingredients — water, heat, and a plumbing system. Melted snow and rain provide the water. This water seeps deep down into the earth. Below the park's surface, there is a pocket of *magma* (hot liquid rock) which heats the water. As the water heats, it rises to the surface through a plumbing system. The plumbing system is a series of cracks and tunnels. Hard *minerals* line these cracks and strengthen them.

The plumbing system and the amount of heat and water determine the type of thermal feature. If hot water rises easily through the plumbing to a surface pool, it forms a <u>hot spring</u> (figure 1). Hot spring pools may bubble or steam.

Look for a special kind of hot spring at Mammoth Hot Springs ❶. At Mammoth, there are beautiful <u>terraced</u> <u>hot</u> <u>springs</u>. This type of spring needs the mineral limestone.

Underground, hot water and carbon dioxide gas combine to form an *acid* solution. This solution dissolves limestone. Rising hot water carries the dissolved limestone to the surface. At the surface, the water pools and flows downhill. The dissolved limestone reforms into a bright white rock called <u>travertine</u>. It is the travertine that builds the growing terraces.

A <u>fumarole</u> is another type of hot spring. The water in this feature never reaches the surface. Instead, the underground water heats until it turns to steam. This steam and some gases rise to the surface. Fumaroles often roar or hiss. This is the sound of steam and gases rushing out of the plumbing system.

A <u>mud pot</u> is a cross between a hot spring and a fumarole. In mud pots, rising gases

FACT OR FICTION: **Water that erupts from geysers comes from rain or snow that fell last year.**

Hurry, Hurry On to Old Faithful!

In general, the water that erupts from geysers fell on Yellowstone hundreds of years earlier. Scientists conducted tests to find out how long it takes water to reach geysers. In one test, they discovered that it took over 500 years for water on Mount Holmes to reach Yellowstone's geysers. (Find Mount Holmes on the map on page 46.) Maybe the geyser spray that showers you today fell as rain when Columbus discovered America. (Now you know the statement is fiction.)

PATTY FURBUSH

Grand Prismatic Spring **18** is the largest hot spring in the park. Besides its size, it is known for its beautiful colors. View the spring from the boardwalk. You'll see a blue haze tinted with rust colors rising above the spring.

make the water acidic. *Acid* dissolves rock and turns it into clay or mud. The mud appears to boil. However, it is the rising steam and gases that cause the mud to bubble. Look for mud pots at Fountain Paint Pot **20**.

There is a distinctive smell at some thermal areas. It is commonly described as rotten eggs. Hydrogen sulfide is the gas responsible for this smell. It is the same gas found in rotten eggs. Visit the Mud Volcano **7** area. Don't let the strong smell keep you from viewing the amazing features. Mud Volcano is a large, explosive mud pot.

The most complex thermal feature is the geyser (figure 2). A geyser is a hot spring that intermittently spouts water and steam.

A geyser's plumbing system is constricted. Far below ground, there is a large cavity (or group of cracks) where heated water gathers. A narrow channel (the constriction) lies between the cavity and the surface. This constriction prevents hot water from rising quickly to the surface where heat can escape. Water in the cavity becomes superheated past the boiling point. However, it cannot boil. The water in the upper plumbing system exerts a pressure on the cavity water that prevents it from boiling.

A small amount of hot water manages to rise up the plumbing system. As it rises, steam bubbles form. The bubbles expand as they rise and push some water from the

figure 1

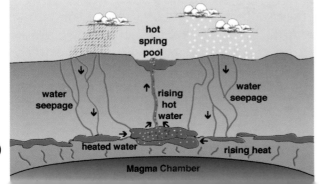

figure 2

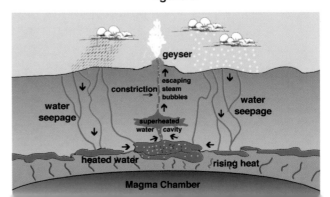

FACT OR FICTION:

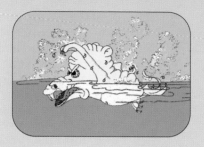

Thermus aquaticus is a deadly creature that lives in Yellowstone's hot springs.

Thermus aquaticus does live in Yellowstone's thermal features. However, it is a beneficial *bacterium*. Scientists created an important *enzyme* from this bacterium. With this enzyme, they diagnose serious medical problems such as AIDS. (Now you know the statement is fiction.)

geyser vent. This decreases the pressure on the heated water below. With the decrease in pressure, the cavity water begins to boil violently. It produces a tremendous amount of steam. Rapidly rising steam forces the water out of the geyser vent in an explosive eruption. The eruption will continue until the geyser expels all the water or until the pressure is relieved.

There are two types of geysers in Yellowstone, fountain-type and cone-type. A gray rocklike deposit called geyserite helps form these two types of geysers. Silica, a crystal-like rock, dissolves in hot underground water. When the water reaches the surface, the silica hardens and forms the geyserite.

Fountain-type geysers spout from a basin of water. Geyserite forms the walls of this basin. When geyserite forms near the mouth of a geyser, it builds into a cone. Water in the cone-type geyser erupts from this cone like a water stream from a hose nozzle.

Look at the geysers in the last chapter. Can you tell which are fountain-type and which are cone-type?

Now that you have read about the thermal features above, try to match their names with the pictures that follow. (Hint: Look for the underlined words in the above text. They are the features pictured.) Walk some trails and see how many different features you can find. Remember to record your findings in your nature notes at the end of the book.

A. This thermal feature is named Daisy ⑮. It intermittently spouts water and steam about every one and one half hours. Daisy is an example of a: _____

Answers:

A.	geyser	F.	fumarole
B.	hot spring	G.	mud pot
C.	terraced hot spring	H.	cone-type
D.	hot springs	I.	travertine
E.	fountain-type	J.	geyserite

B. 🖎 Water easily rises to the surface in Morning Glory Pool ⑮. This pool got its name because it resembles the color and shape of a morning glory flower.

Thoughtless people have thrown debris into the pool, clogging the vent. As a result, the pool has lost some of its brilliant color.

What type of thermal feature is Morning Glory Pool?

_____

C. ☝ This special kind of hot spring forms when the *mineral* limestone is present. This feature is called a: _____

D. Emerald Pool ⑯ (above) and Sapphire Pool ⑰ (below) are both examples of _____.
The emerald green is the result of yellow *algae* growing in the deep blue water (yellow + blue = green). The brilliant sapphire blue is due to the reflection of skylight.

PHOTOS BY PATTY FURBUSH

MICHAEL H. FRANCIS

G.  Rising steam and gases make this feature appear to boil. _____

H. You will find Lone Star Geyser ⑭ at the end of a short bike and foot trail. This predictable geyser erupts about every three hours. Which type of geyser is Lone Star?

_____

E. Cliff Geyser ⑯ sits on the edge of the Firehole River. This geyser erupts frequently from a pool of water. Which type of geyser is Cliff Geyser? _____

F. Water never reaches the surface in this feature. Listen for the roaring and hissing sounds of gas and steam rushing out of the vent. This feature is a: _____

I. Minerva Terrace at Mammoth Hot Springs ① is a terraced hot spring. The white rock mineral that creates the terraces is called _____. The terraces are covered with color — oranges, pinks, yellows, greens, and browns. Masses of living *bacteria* and *algae* create these colors.

PHOTOS BY PATTY FURBUSH

J. In Upper Geyser Basin ⑮, you'll find Crested Pool. Water temperatures in this hot spring exceed 199° F. The water boils almost constantly. Note the rock-like rim that surrounds the pool. This gray deposit is called

THE GEOLOGIC STORY

There is more to Yellowstone than geysers and hot springs. Other amazing geologic features include large lakes, deep canyons, and spectacular waterfalls. Yellowstone also has *petrified* trees and a volcano *caldera*. A geologic story connects all these features.

Two million years ago, volcanic eruptions showered Yellowstone with ash and rock. Huge ash and *lava* (hot liquid rock) flows covered much of the area. This volcanic activity created some of the mountains in the park.

About 600,000 years ago, there was another violent volcanic period. Several forceful eruptions occurred in a matter of minutes.

Massive amounts of ash, rock, and *magma* exploded from the ground beneath Yellowstone. These eruptions emptied a huge underground chamber.

The thin earthen roof of this chamber collapsed creating a giant *basin* called a caldera. Later volcanic activity filled much of the caldera making a volcanic *plateau*. Today, you can still see part of the caldera rim.

Volcanic flows are responsible for different rock types. Some flows cooled to form rhyolite, the most common type of rock in the park. In western Yellowstone, *lava* cooled quickly to form a smooth, glassy rock called obsidian. Look for this rock at Obsidian Cliff ㉓, sometimes called a "Mountain of Glass".

Part of the Yellowstone *caldera* filled with water and created Yellowstone Lake (below). More recent (150,000 years ago) volcanic eruptions in West Thumb ⑪ enlarged the lake and made it deeper. Visit West Thumb and see the thermal features on the edge of the lake.

MICHAEL H. FRANCIS

Some ash and lava flows cooled to form *basalt* columns. Look for these columns near Sheepeater Cliff and Tower Fall 4 . At Sheepeater Cliff 24 (below), look for an ascending series of columns. Do you think this is a natural occurrence? Or did the Sheepeater Indians make a stone staircase to get up the cliff?

One lava flow became part of a beautiful geologic wonder — the Grand Canyon of the Yellowstone 6 . This volcanic flow hardened and formed a ribbon of rhyolite rock. Thermal features developed in the hardened flow. Hot steam and gases weakened the rhyolite, making it easy to *erode*. Rivers flowed over the lava ribbon and washed the weak rock away. A canyon began to form. For thousands of years, the river has continued to carve the canyon deeper and deeper.

There are two spectacular waterfalls within the Grand Canyon of the Yellowstone.

Erosion helped create Upper (109' high) and Lower (308' high) falls. Erosion has occurred more quickly at the bottom of the falls than at the top.

Look for *thermal* steam in the canyon below the falls. This thermal activity weakens rock at the base of the falls. The river can easily erode the weak rock. The harder rock above the falls is more resistant to erosion.

Check out the "Fact or Fiction" boxes and picture captions to learn more about Yellowstone's amazing geology.

FACT OR FICTION:

The Continental Divide is a chain of the highest mountains in the country.

The Continental Divide is a continuous ridge of high points. This ridge divides the North American Continent into two watersheds. The water that falls on the east side of the ridge travels to the Atlantic Ocean. Water that falls on the west side eventually ends up in the Pacific Ocean.

Although the Continental Divide is high, it does not contain all the highest points in the United States. There are other peaks that are higher. For example, Mt. Whitney in California is the highest mountain in the country (not counting Alaska). It's not part of the Continental Divide. All water that falls on Mt. Whitney travels to the Pacific Ocean. Which side of the divide will you find Mt. Whitney? (Now you know the statement is fiction.)

PHOTOS BY PATTY FURBUSH

Isa Lake straddles the Continental Divide. When water levels are high, the lake water flows to both the Pacific and Atlantic Oceans. Look for Isa Lake as you drive over the Continental Divide at Craig Pass ⑬.

The wonderful colors are an inspiring feature of the Grand Canyon of the Yellowstone ⑥. Grays, pinks, and lavenders are the natural colors of rhyolite rock. Rhyolite stained with iron compounds creates the beautiful shades of orange and yellow.

FACT OR FICTION:

Yellowstone Lake is the largest mountain lake in the United States.

There are many lakes in the country larger than Yellowstone Lake. However, Yellowstone Lake's size and location do make it famous. It is the largest high altitude lake in the United States. It lies at 7,733 feet in elevation. The water surface covers 136 square miles. It has 110 miles of shoreline. (Now you know the statement is fact.)

Caldera Rim   Gallatin Mountains   Porcupine Hills

Yellowstone's volcanic *caldera* measures about 28 miles from north to south and 47 miles in width. It is one of the world's largest calderas. You can see the caldera rim in several places throughout the park. This view of the caldera rim is from Fountain Paint Pots ㉑.

Volcanic ash and mud flows are responsible for a geologic curiosity — *petrified* trees. Millions of years ago, volcanic ash buried trees in the Yellowstone area. The ash contained silica, a crystal-like rock. A solution of silica and water seeped into the dead trees. The silica solution filled each tree cell then hardened into rock. The result was petrified trees — exact stone copies of the dead trees. Stop to see the petrified tree ② on the Grand Loop. It's on a side road, west of Tower Junction. Below: The remains of three standing petrified trees dwarf a hiker in Yellowstone's backcountry.

PHOTOS BY PATTY FURBUSH

☞ Lower Falls of the Grand Canyon of the Yellowstone. Trails lead to the top of the falls and down into the canyon. If you like stairs, try Uncle Tom's Trail. Over 300 steps lead down to an excellent viewpoint.

WONDERFUL WILDLIFE

Yellowstone is well known for its abundant wildlife. The park has the largest concentration of mammals in the United States (not counting Alaska). There are over 300 species of animals. This includes 60 mammals, 9 reptiles and amphibians, 18 fish, and over 225 birds.

It's not just the numbers but the kinds of animals that make the park famous. Animals threatened with *extinction* have found a safe home in Yellowstone. One of these animals is the grizzly bear. Yellowstone is one of the last homes for this *threatened* species.

Bison, once near extinction, now number about 4,000 in the park. The trumpeter swan has also come back from near extinction. It nests in some areas of the park. In 1995, the National Park Service reintroduced wolves to the park. From 1930 to 1995, there were no wolves in the park.

At Yellowstone, you can see wildlife throughout the year. However, the animals are more visible in the spring and fall. In mid summer, many elk and bison move up to high country. During winter, some animals enter a long *hibernation* or deep sleep. Other animals *migrate* away from the park to escape the cold and snow. But even in mid winter, you'll find wildlife in Yellowstone. Look for bison and elk near the thermal basins. In thermal areas, heat melts the snow making it easier for wildlife to find food.

FACT OR FICTION:

It's time to trade in our horns.

Moose and bighorn sheep shed their horns each year and grow new ones.

Bighorn Sheep have large curved horns. Horns grow throughout an animal's life. They do not fall off.

A moose is a member of the deer family. All male deer grow antlers, not horns. Deer shed their antlers every year in late winter or spring. New antlers begin to grow as soon as the old ones fall.

A soft velvet-like skin covers the new, growing antlers. This velvet contains blood vessels that bring calcium and *minerals* for making strong antler bone. Antlers reach full size in about 3 months. Some antlers may grow as much as 2 inches a day. In late summer, deer rub the velvet off to expose the fully grown antlers. (Now you know the statement is fiction.)

The gray wolf used to be common in Yellowstone. However, people thought wolves threatened other wildlife. The government started a program that exterminated the wolf by 1930. Since then, people have learned that wolves have an important role in nature. They help keep other animal populations in balance. In 1995, the government reintroduced wolves to Yellowstone. Now there are several wolf packs in the park.

Is the wolf dangerous to people? Healthy wolves have never seriously injured a person. Wolves use their sharp teeth for hunting wild animals such as elk.

Wolves live and hunt in groups called packs. Each pack has one dominant male and female wolf. These two wolves, called alphas, rule the pack. They are the only wolves that mate and have young.

As you travel through the park, look and listen. Try to identify some of the animals. These pictures will help you. Record your findings in your nature notes at the end of the book.

MICHAEL H. FRANCIS

Trumpeter swans are among the rarest waterfowl in the country. They are the heaviest wild bird in North America. Yellowstone is one of the few places where these swans nest. Look for them along the Madison River.

Unlike other waterfowl which *migrate* south, some trumpeters stay in Yellowstone year round. These swans have glands that secrete oil. The oil covers the birds' feathers and insulates them against Yellowstone's cold winters.

21

MICHAEL H. FRANCIS

MICHAEL H. FRANCIS

MICHAEL S. SAMPLE

FACT OR FICTION:
The wapiti is a small water animal that is now extinct.

Is the grizzly bear a terrible beast? It can stand seven feet high. Its claws can grow up to six inches (about the size of a pen). Forty-two teeth line its mouth. (How many teeth do you have?) At a speed of 30 mph, it can outrun any person.

The grizzly may seem frightening, but it is usually not aggressive. It eats mostly plants, wild fruits, insects, rodents, and *carrion*. The grizzly doesn't use its claws, sharp teeth, and strong muscles for hunting large animals. It uses them for digging up rodents and defending itself against other bears.

Sometimes the grizzly is fierce and unpredictable. A mother bear aggressively protects her cubs. Surprised bears may attack if they feel threatened. Most bears will fight to protect their food.

Here are some tips to avoid encounters with grizzlies. View grizzly bears from a long distance. Hike in groups and make noise to avoid surprising a bear. Stay away from areas where bears are feeding.

The wapiti (*wahp'-i-tee*) is the American Indian name for elk. In Shawnee, it means "white rump". Elk are one of the largest members of the deer family. A male elk can stand 5 feet at the shoulder. It can weigh up to 1000 pounds.

Elk are numerous in many areas of the western states. Yellowstone has a larger population of elk than any other place in the world. (Now you know the statement is fiction.)

☛ Bighorn Sheep were once numerous. Now, they only live in remote mountain areas. They are usually difficult to see. Their tan coat helps them blend in with their rocky habitat. They can stand perfectly still for long periods. (Try it.)

Bighorn sheep have an amazing ability to travel over steep mountain cliffs. They have concave feet with spongy pads that help them grip the rock. Clinging to the cliff, they may look as if they are in danger. However, they are quite at ease in their steep, rocky home.

The largest land mammal in North America is the bison. A bison can be six feet at the shoulder and weigh as much as a small car. Sixty million of these animals once roamed the plains. Because of hunting and expanding civilization, the bison disappeared. In the late 1800's, there were less than 25 wild bison in Yellowstone. This small herd found a refuge in a remote part of the park. Today bison are numerous. There are about 4000 roaming the grasslands of Yellowstone's valleys.

Bison look slow and tame; however, they can quickly change their disposition. They can run at speeds up to 40 mph. (Man's fastest running speed is about 12-15 mph.) Don't get close to a bison. It may suddenly decide it doesn't want you near. It might charge you or gore you with its horns.

PHOTOS BY PATTY FURBUSH

Canada geese: largest of all wild geese

☞ An osprey has amazing eyesight. It can see fish in the water from 100 feet in the air. Ospreys catch fish by plunging feet first into the water. They hang on to slippery fish with large claws and sharp spines on their feet. Look for osprey nests in the Grand Canyon of the Yellowstone ⑥. You'll find them high on the cliffs.

Male elk antlers may weigh up to 50 lbs. (Imagine carrying these heavy antlers on your head.) Velvet covers the antlers while they are growing. In late summer, the elk rub the velvet off to expose hard, sharp antlers. Now the elk are ready to fight each other. The winner becomes the leader of a herd.

Fall is a great time to visit elk country. That's when the elk bugle. This beautiful, but eerie sound, can be described as a cross between a flute and a whistle. ☜ bull (male) elk

23

☞ The cutthroat trout is the only trout native to Yellowstone. Trout will often travel upstream to breed in the place where they hatched. Each female fish may lay up to 10,000 eggs.

☞ Moose are the largest and most powerful members of the deer family. They have long legs for wading in Yellowstone's marshes and ponds.

MICHAEL H. FRANCIS

☝ A small island in Yellowstone Lake is one of the few breeding places in the world for white pelicans. Both parents raise their young on this remote island. Look for white pelicans near Fishing Bridge ⑧. Watch them in flight. You can identify them by their black wingtips.

☝ America's fastest land animal is the pronghorn.

NATIONAL PARK SERVICE

☝ The coyote is one of the park's most important predators. It helps keep rodent populations in balance. Watch for a coyote leaping in a field as it tries to catch small animals.

☝ Yellow-bellied marmots live on Yellowstone's grassy hillsides. They make their burrows in rocky areas. When disturbed, marmots make a shrill whistle call. This has prompted their nickname, whistlepig.

☞ Unlike grizzlies, black bears have short claws and are good tree climbers. A mother bear will often shoo her cubs up a tree when she senses danger.

HABITATS & ECOSYSTEMS

A number of plant communities support the animal life in Yellowstone. A plant community occurs when a variety of plants grow together under similar conditions. These communities provide different *habitats* for animals.

Wetland habitats include areas around rivers, streams, ponds, and marshes. This is the place to find moose, beaver, swans, and ducks. Elk and bison graze on the lush grasses growing near the water's edge.

Flat meadows and open, rolling hills provide another type of habitat. Grasses are abundant in these areas. In dry open areas, sagebrush is common. Open areas are favorite places for elk, bison, pronghorn, and sage grouse. Meadows are a great place to view grizzly bears from a distance.

Forest habitats cover much of Yellowstone. These forests include lodgepole pine, spruce and fir, and Douglas fir forests. Birds, bears, squirrels, and chipmunks enjoy forest habitats. Other animals use the forests to sleep in or to find shade.

In mountain habitats, yellow-bellied marmots scamper through high rocky meadows. Bighorn sheep graze upon alpine tundra.

Alpine tundra is a plant community that thrives above treeline in high mountains. The plants growing on these peaks can survive the worst of

PHOTOS BY PATTY FURBUSH

The fringed gentian is Yellowstone National Park's official flower. It flowers throughout the summer.

Indian paintbrush
Wyoming State Flower

Mother Nature's snow, wind, and cold. They are fragile plants that take many years to grow.

Hydrothermal areas create a unique habitat. It's a habitat that supports tiny organisms. At first look, thermal basins seem lifeless. However, these hot spots contain more life than the other habitats combined. Look at the colors and you will find life. Green, yellow, orange, red, and brown. These are the colors of the *algae* and *bacteria* that live in hot water. An individual *alga* or *bacterium* is microscopic (invisible to the human eye). However, millions of these organisms group together to make the colorful mats surrounding thermal features.

Aspen trees grow in small groves scattered throughout grasslands and forests. The leaves tremble with even a light breeze. This trembling is what prompted the common name of this tree — quaking aspen. Helianthella flowers abound in this meadow near the aspens.

FACT OR FICTION:

Indian paintbrush flowers can be red, magenta, orange, or yellow.

The Indian paintbrush can be all the colors above. However, it is the colored bract leaves that make the paintbrush so beautiful. The actual flowers are greenish-yellow. (Now you know the statement is fiction.)

Native Americans have a legend about how this plant got its name. A young Indian was trying to paint the sunset. He became frustrated and threw down his brushes. Where the brushes landed, beautiful plants sprang up. The plants were all the colors of a sunset.

As you travel through Yellowstone, look for the variety of Indian paintbrush colors. How many sunset colors can you find?

Different types of these organisms live in different water temperatures. Look for white and yellow bacteria strands. These *thermal* bacteria grow in the hottest water. As water cools, yellow, orange, and green bacteria thrive. Dark oranges, browns, and greens signal the water has cooled even more.

Many animals depend upon the hydrothermal habitat. Insects and spiders live in or on the edge of bacterial mats. These insects are food for birds. Larger animals seek out hydrothermal habitat for its warmth.

As you travel through Yellowstone, pick out the different habitats. Note the animals you see in each habitat.

PHOTOS BY PATTY FURBUSH

Look for the Lewis monkeyflower (reddish-purple) while traveling over Dunraven Pass ⑤. The mountain bluebell (purplish-blue) blooms in July and August.

Colorful flowers grow on high mountain tops. Sky pilot (purple) and groundsel (yellow) grow along the Mount Washburn ⑤ trail.

Shake Hands With An Evergreen

An evergreen is a tree that stays green year round. Most evergreens in the park are lodgepole pine trees. However, there are other evergreens such as Douglas fir, subalpine fir, and Engelmann spruce. It can be difficult to tell the difference between evergreens by looking at them. But shake hands with a branch, and the tree will introduce itself.

A spruce will be sharp and prickly on your hand. Roll one of the spruce's short needles between your fingers. Spruce starts with "S". Spruce needles are sharp and square.

A fir will be friendly to your hand. Try to roll a needle between your fingers. Fir starts with "F". Fir needles are flat and friendly.

Lodgepole pine needles are very different. They are longer and grouped in bundles of two. Look at a complete pine needle bundle and notice that it is round. Look at a single needle and note that it is flat on one side and round on the other.

An easy flower to identify is the pond lily or wokus (American Indian name). It is the only large yellow flower floating on Yellowstone's waters.

Lupine (blue) and sticky geraniums (pink) are common in open areas. Lupine is a favorite food for forest animals.

The leaves of the sticky geranium give this plant its name. Sticky hairs cover the leaves.

27

Below: Look closely at the elephanthead. Each little flower resembles the head of an elephant, complete with trunk and ears. It grows in wet areas.

☞ Cow parsnip (white) is easy to identify. It has 4-6 inch wide flower clusters. Bear, elk, and deer eat the stems and leaves of this plant. Helianthella (yellow) is just one of the many types of sunflowers that grow in the park.

PHOTOS BY PATTY FURBUSH

☞ Colorful *bacteria* grows in the hot run-off water from Punchbowl Spring. (Upper Geyser Basin ⑮.)

Formula For An Ecosystem

An ecosystem has everything nature needs to support a complex group of plants and animals. Within an ecosystem, there are several habitats and plant and animal communities.

Yellowstone is part of a large ecosystem. By itself, Yellowstone cannot protect all life within its boundaries. There are no fences to keep animals in the park. Bison, grizzlies, and wolves wander outside the park boundaries. Elk herds *migrate* to the forests and National Wildlife Refuge near Jackson, WY. These animals need protection outside the park too.

Thermal features also need extra protection. *Hydrothermal* features might be connected to water sources outside the park. If people overuse water sources near the park, they may be taking water that feeds Yellowstone's geysers.

Land managers developed the Greater Yellowstone Ecosystem to help protect the life and features of Yellowstone. This ecosystem includes Yellowstone and Grand Teton national parks, two national wildlife refuges, six national forests, public, state, and private lands. Managers of these areas work together to prevent misuse of *natural resources*. Hopefully the life and features at Yellowstone will stay as abundant and complex as nature designed.

FIRE — NATURE'S TOOL

Long before people came to Yellowstone, there were fires. Lightning caused most of these fires. Major fires have occurred every 300 to 400 years. The 1988 Yellowstone fires were part of that natural cycle.

The summer of 1988 started out wet. But as summer progressed, it became dryer and dryer. The usual summer rains never arrived. It became the driest summer in the park's history. Then the fires started.

For nature, this was just another part of the natural cycle. However, for many people who loved Yellowstone, the fires were scary. They saw this cherished park going up in flame. It was being "destroyed". People had not seen this massive amount of fire power before.

When the fires were over, there seemed to be blackness everywhere. Once lush green meadows and forests looked dead and bar-

Firefighters worked hard to put out the 1988 fires. It was the largest firefighting effort in United States history. Firefighters saved many buildings and special areas; but, they could not stop all the forest fires. It was the September snows that finally put out all the fires.

JEFF & ALEXA HENRY

FACT OR FICTION:

Forest Fires help lodgepole pines to reseed.

Jump seeds! Our cone's on fire!

Lodgepole pines have two kinds of cones. Pine pitch seals one type of cone closed. It only opens up when the heat of fire melts the pitch. Once the cone is open, the seeds inside can fall to the ground. This type of cone ensures that lodgepole pines will reseed after a forest fire.

Lodgepole trees have a second type of cone that opens regularly. It drops seeds to the ground without the help of fire. Lodgepole pines can reseed with or without fire. (Now you know the statement is fact.)

ren. Why did this have to happen to this spectacular land? People wondered throughout the winter. Then spring came.

New green plants sprouted among the dead trees and ashes. The fire had not destroyed the park. It had helped a new life cycle begin. The fires killed many trees; however, new life grew almost everywhere the fire burned.

Visitors to Yellowstone today are lucky to experience this new life cycle. They can see how the fires created open sunlit areas and stimulated the growth of lush vegetation.

At Grant Visitor Center ⑫, exhibits explain fire's effect on nature. Walk around the center and learn how fire tidies up and fertilizes the forest floor. At the center, you'll also discover how fires seed new forests and create new habitat for wildlife.

When you visit Yellowstone, look among the dead, fire-killed trees. See the new life that grows from the ashes. Fireweed (below) is just one of the many colorful flowers that quickly spread through burned areas.

JEFF & ALEXA HENRY

FROM COLTER'S HELL TO NATIONAL PARK

To some early Native Americans, Yellowstone's land of boiling mud and water seemed "possessed by spirits." Many believed the unusual thermal activity was a warning to stay away. Some natives camped in the area as they traveled through on hunting expeditions. However, they did not live in Yellowstone.

There was one exception. A small band of Shoshoni Indians lived in Yellowstone year round. These Indians ate mainly fish and bighorn sheep. They were called Sheepeaters.

The first White Man to visit the area was John Colter. Around 1807, he traveled through the area trying to improve trade with Native Americans. He returned to civilization with stories of Yellowstone's wonders. People called his stories tall tales. They didn't believe these stories until organized expeditions came back from Yellowstone.

The year 1869 began the era of *expeditions*. Members of the expeditions decided that Yellowstone should be protected and kept free from settlement. The 1871 Hayden expedition was one of the most important expeditions. Artist, Thomas Moran, and photographer, William H. Jackson, accompanied this expedition. They captured Yellowstone's wonders in picture.

Photographs, paintings, a written report, and information from earlier expeditions provided the backing for a park *bill*. The bill was presented to Congress and passed. In 1872, President Grant signed the bill creating the world's first national park — Yellowstone National Park!

Yellowstone did not get instant protection. *Natural resource* destruction plagued the early years of the park. Poaching (illegal killing of wildlife) was a big problem. Visitors chipped apart geyser formations to get souvenirs.

In 1886, Congress realized they had to take action. They assigned the U. S. Army

FACT OR FICTION: Sheepeater Indians used the horn of a bighorn to catch bighorn sheep.

Sheepeater Indians discovered that the horns of bighorn sheep became flexible when heated. The Indians stretched the heated horn into a three-foot long bow. After it cooled, the bow stiffened. This bow became the Sheepeaters' principal weapon for hunting bighorn sheep. (Now you know the statement is fact.)

MINI MYSTERY: TALL TALES?

Read about a real mountain man, Jim Bridger. Then test your detective skills.

Tom Warren was excited. His cavalry troop was going west to Fort Laramie.

"They say it's beautiful country, Mother. There are mountains bigger than you can imagine."

Tom's mother did not share his excitement. She worried about her son's safety. In the 1860's, the western frontier was full of uncertainties.

"I don't suppose anyone told you about the dangers," said Mrs. Warren with concern.

"Don't worry, Mother. We'll have a great guide. They say Jim Bridger is the best mountaineer, trapper, and tracker in the country."

"What about the Indians?" Mrs. Warren asked.

"Everyone says Mr. Bridger has courage and good judgment," Tom explained. "He can talk to about a dozen Indian tribes in their own tongue. And he is a master of sign language."

"I feel better knowing you have a good guide," Mrs. Warren sighed. "But, I'll still worry."

"Please, don't worry." Tom tried to comfort his mother. "Think about the exciting things I will see. Jim told us of a giant fountain that spouts water over a hundred feet into the air. It spouts every hour. Then there's the bathing river. Once a day, a shower of hot water shoots over a river. The falling water turns the cold river water into bath water. Jim saw a huge hole filled with boiling mud. If you stand too close, you will get a mud pie in the face. He said..."

"It sounds like your expert guide is also an expert at tall tales," interrupted Mrs. Warren.

"Mother, I'm sure it's true," said Tom. "Look. There's Mr. Bridger over at the livery stable. Come, I want you to meet him."

Tom and his mother walked to the stables.

"Excuse me, sir," said Tom. "I'd like you to meet my mother."

"Howdy, ma'am," said Jim.

"Tom has told me much about you, Mr. Bridger. You must be a very capable guide. And I'm sure you'll keep the men entertained with your stories of great fountains," Mrs. Warren said with a smile.

"Why, Mrs. Warren! It sounds as if ya don't believe my stories," Jim exclaimed.

Jim thought to himself. "Everyone has a hard time believing about the land of boiling water. I'll have some fun with her. I'll tell her some real tall tales."

"Ma'am, let me tell you more of the Western Wonders," Jim began. "Once I fired my rifle at a bull elk. The elk did not even raise his head. I crawled up as near as I dared and fired three more times. Still the elk did not move. I grabbed my rifle like a club and charged the elk. I stopped short, crashing into a mountain of clear glass. I found out the mountain was like a telescope lens. The elk was actually 25 miles away."

Mrs. Warren laughed. "That's a mountain I'd go west to see, Mr. Bridger."

"Oh, I've got to tell you about the peetrified forests. I found peetrified trees agrowin' with peetrified birds on them singin' peetrified songs. Even the moon shines with peetrified light."

By now, Tom was bursting with laughter. Mrs. Warren also laughed. Her worries seemed to melt away.

Mrs. Warren gave Jim Bridger a large smile. "I'll still worry about my son, but I am glad you will be guiding him with your good care and humor."

"I promise to do my best, ma'am." Jim gave Mrs. Warren a hearty handshake and a big smile.

Look for Mystery Questions on page 33.

The National Hotel (right) was the first hotel in the park. The Northern Pacific Railroad built it in the late 1800's. Early visitors usually came to Yellowstone by railroad. From the railroad depot in Gardiner, Montana, they boarded a six-horse stagecoach. The stagecoach took them to their first stop, the National Hotel. This hotel was the starting point for park tours.

The National Hotel was torn down in 1936. The present hotel, Mammoth Hot Springs Hotel  was built on the same site. Visit the Map Room in the hotel. You'll find a giant antique map of the United States. It was made from 15 types of wood from 9 different countries.

NATIONAL PARK SERVICE

to protect Yellowstone. The army worked out of Fort Yellowstone, which they built at Mammoth ①. The army also built several small stations throughout the park. Soldiers patrolled the park and helped stop vandalism.

Yellowstone attracted many tourists. They came from all over the world as they still do today. The early visitors usually arrived on the Northern Pacific Railroad. The railroad provided food and lodging in the park.

During these early days, the railroad built the park's famous hotels —National Hotel, Old Faithful Inn ⑮, and the Lake Hotel ⑨.

A major change began in 1916 when Congress created the National Park Service. Congress charged this new agency with protecting all national parks. Soon after its creation, the National Park Service replaced the army. Today, the National Park Service still protects the world's first national park.

PATTY FURBUSH

There are many historical Fort Yellowstone buildings at Mammoth ①. The visitor center is in what used to be the Bachelor Officers' Quarters. The National Park Service uses the fort's enlisted barracks for an administrative building (left).

Visit the Ranger Museum at Norris ㉒. It Is in one of the original soldier stations. The museum has exhibits that explain the evolution of the ranger from early military days to present day.

Mini Mystery Questions: 1. Which stories of Yellowstone's features were tall tales? 2. Which were facts about Yellowstone features? 3. Which features was Jim referring to when he told of a fountain that spouts every hour, of a fountain that spouts daily over a river, and of boiling mud? 4. Where in Yellowstone is Bridger's glass mountain? 5. Is there any truth in the peetrified story? *Answers on page 44*

The Lake Hotel is the oldest existing hotel in the park. In 1891, it opened for guests. Additions to the hotel have made it the longest wood hotel in the world — 890' long. Pillars, gables, and balconies were added to the hotel in the early 1900's. This prompted the hotel's second name, the Colonial Hotel.

Some of the early hotel guests arrived at the hotel aboard the steamboat "Zillah". They would board the boat at West Thumb. Other guests arrived by coach. In those days, the hotels catered to the wealthy. Formal dress was required. The cost of $4.00 a night was expensive.

FACT OR FICTION: The beautiful curved and knotted poles in the Old Faithful Inn are imported cypress logs.

The primary materials used to build Old Faithful Inn came from the local area. The stone was quarried from a hill located just 5 miles away. The lodgepole walls were from nearby forests. The twisted and knotted log supports were harder to find. However, even these logs came from forests in or near the park. The knots and twists are the result of a *bacterial* formation in the branches and trunks of lodgepole pines.

The Inn was built before the National Park Service had regulations. Today, it is illegal to gather building materials inside the park. (Now you know the statement is fiction.)

PHOTOS BY PATTY FURBUSH

When the Old Faithful Inn was completed in 1904, it was the world's largest log hotel. The magnificent lobby rises 85 feet — seven stories high. Four overhanging balconies overlook the lobby. A massive stone fireplace stands three stories high.

The original Old Faithful Inn had 140 rooms. With the addition of two wings by 1928, the number of rooms increased to 370.

Much of the initial construction was done in the middle of winter. Wander around the Inn. Imagine being a builder on a cold December morning in 1903. What hardships the builders must have endured to create this magnificent structure.

A GREAT PLACE TO VISIT

Yellowstone is one of the largest national parks in the United States. It is larger than the states of Delaware and Rhode Island combined. With 2.2 million acres, Yellowstone has much to offer for recreation. To appreciate the park, you should stay at least three days.

Park roads travel around a loop of the park highlights. This 142 mile loop is called the Grand Loop. You can travel this loop in a day. However, that's not enough time to stop and enjoy the park. It is better to travel slowly and stop often. Many books offer a mile by mile guide to the Grand Loop.

Take a walk on the nature trails. There are seven self-guided nature trails — Mammoth Hot Springs ①, Norris Geyser Basin ㉒, West Thumb Geyser Basin ⑪, Upper Geyser Basin ⑮, Canyon ⑥, Fountain Paint Pot ⑳/ Firehole Lake Drive ⑲, and Mud Volcano ⑦. These areas have pamphlets that describe the features. In addition, there are other trails that have signs along the way. Rangers give talks and walks around many of these areas. Check a visitor center for a schedule of programs.

There are over 1000 miles of trail in the park. Most trails lead through wilderness. People who want to experience this wilderness can get a backpacking permit. This allows them to camp in the wilderness, away from roads.

For those who want to camp closer to civilization, there are twelve campgrounds.

The hike up Mt. Washburn ⑤ is one of the most popular wilderness hikes in the park. Trails ascend about 2.5 miles to a lookout tower. The mountain top is in alpine tundra area. Remember to stay on the trails as alpine plants are fragile.

Five of these are available by reservation. There are also many cabins, lodges, and hotel rooms available by reservation.

Watching for wildlife is a favorite activity in Yellowstone. People line the road pullouts in the park valleys. They scan the meadows for a glimpse of a wolf or grizzly. To see a wolf or bear is a special treat. But you don't have to look long to see other wildlife including bison, elk, squirrels, mar-

Concessions offer many fun ways to see the park. At Roosevelt Lodge ③, you can catch a stagecoach. Board a replica (copy) of a stagecoach used by the early park visitors. Ride over a dirt road and imagine you are touring the park in the early 1900's.

Other concession activities are wagon ride cookouts and horseback trail rides. Outfitters offer overnight horse pack trips into the backcountry.

At Bridge Bay ⑩, you can rent boats from a concession or set out on a scenic boat cruise across Yellowstone Lake.

PHOTOS BY PATTY FURBUSH

mots, and birds. You'll find these animals throughout the park.

A great way to learn about the park is to go to the visitor centers. There are six major centers. Each center has a different theme. Grant Visitor Center ⑫ emphasizes fire ecology. Fishing Bridge ⑧ has exhibits on animal life in Yellowstone, particularly around the lake. At Old Faithful ⑮, there are films and programs about geysers. Albright Visitor Center at Mammoth ① has exhibits on the park's history and wildlife.

Visit Norris Visitor Center ㉒ to see exhibits on thermal features and life surrounding these features. Don't forget the Ranger Museum at Norris Campground. Exhibits there explain how the guardians of Yellowstone changed from volunteer to army to National Park Service.

Canyon Visitor Center ⑥ has exhibits that periodically change. Sometimes it's devoted to Art in Yellowstone. Other times the theme is bison. Stop in and see what's new. You'll find other smaller information stations throughout the park.

The Junior Ranger Program is a great opportunity for children ages 5-12. Junior Rangers learn about the park and complete activities in Yellowstone's Junior Ranger Paper. After completing the program, a ranger presents them with a badge. Earn a Junior Ranger badge and wear it with pride.

JEFF & ALEXA HENRY

Yellowstone National Park is a famous fishing destination. Rivers like the Madison (left) and the Yellowstone (right) are well known around the world. If you are under age sixteen, you can get a free fishing permit from any ranger station. Adults can get a permit for a small fee. Yellowstone's native fish include cutthroat trout, graylings, and whitefish.

Try your luck at fly fishing! Using a fly rod involves a rhythmic back and forth whipping of the fishing line. To avoid getting the line tangled, fishermen often wade into the water. Look for fly fishermen (and women) as you travel along the park waterways.

☞ There are 15 bicycle trails in the park. These trails provide a great way to travel to quieter areas of the park. Cars are not allowed on these trails. They are open only to bicycle and foot traffic. The trails range from one-half mile to five miles in length.

☞ The Old Faithful Snow Lodge ⑮ stays open for winter visitors. Many people travel into the park on specially designed snow coaches.

Winter visitors enjoy skiing and snowmobiling on snow-covered roads. There are numerous marked trails for cross-country skiing.

PHOTOS BY PATTY FURBUSH

MICHAEL H. FRANCIS

☞ Rangers provide programs throughout the park. In this wolf program, the ranger invites visitors to touch. Other types of programs include hikes, walks, and films. Campers particularly enjoy evening campfire programs. Rangers present these programs nightly at outside theaters.

FACT OR FICTION:

You can get so close to Yellowstone's wildlife that it is like being at the zoo.

Many of Yellowstone's animals look tame. Some don't seem to care if you walk up to them. But remember, these are wild animals. There are no fences between you and them. Wild animals can be unpredictable and change their disposition without notice.

The National Park Service requires that people stay at least 25 yards away from most wildlife. You must stay at least 100 yards (length of a football field) away from bears. Bears, elk, and bison have injured many people who have ignored this regulation.

Because there are no fences, Yellowstone is not like a zoo. (Now you know the statement is fiction.)

37

PHOTOS BY PATTY FURBUSH

**A great way to experience Yellowstone is to find a quiet place.
Just sit, look, and listen. Discover this amazing Wonderland!**

Gaze in wonder at the largest concentration of geysers in the world. Hear nature's power thundering over waterfalls in the Grand Canyon of the Yellowstone. Travel through the great variety and abundance of plants and animals. Know that animals once threatened with *extinction* have found a safe home in the park. Sense the vastness of the park. Drive into three states and cross the continental divide three times. View the result of forest fires and understand its role in nature. Indeed, Yellowstone is a remarkable place. No wonder it's the world's first and most famous national park.

Yellowstone is protected so everyone can enjoy this special place. We can be thankful that the early expeditions inspired Congress to preserve this land of amazing features. Now it's up to you. Enjoy and discover Yellowstone National Park. Be sure to take good care of it. Remember this is your Wonderland. This is your National Park!

Word Search: Wildlife Record Holders

Answer the following clues about record holding animals that live in the park. Then circle your answers in the word search puzzle. The answers to the clues can be found in the word list at the bottom of the page. All the animals in the word list are in the word search puzzle. To make the puzzle more challenging, try to answer the clues without looking at the word list.

1. Yellowstone has the largest concentration of this animal in the world. _____
2. Largest bear in the lower 48 states _____
3. Largest and most powerful member of the deer family _____
4. America's fastest land animal _____
5. Largest land mammal in North America _____
6. Heaviest wild bird in North America _____
7. Largest of all wild geese _____
8. One of the fastest swimmers in the animal kingdom - <u>otter</u>
9. Considered by some to be the most intelligent bird in North America - <u>raven</u>
10. Largest rodent in North America - <u>beaver</u>
11. Largest cat in North America - <u>mountain lion</u>
12. Smallest bird in North America - <u>Calliope hummingbird</u>

Answers: page 44

```
M O U N T A I N L I O N G W R A K F M O M F D F E E L Q
T W H I T E P E L I C A N G O Y K G E O V I Z D J K X Q
V R Y T Q G M I R W H T E V D L F U V S O W L D J F M C
E X U R G Y D A A T I Q D T M B F F R T J S J P W O R J
J F M M O R U W V K H P Z B I G H O R N S H E E P B V N
F Q I R P D I N E O D F M A G P I E P R O N G H O R N H
X T R Y J E V Z N C A L L I O P E H U M M I N G B I R D
M A R M O T T O Z F Z O A M X Y E L K A X W S Y C E K D
X I F X Z G U E D L F B E A V E R Z E F R G L I H I B H
M U L E D E E R R Y Y Z J Z V Q H E Y E Y M X B I S O N
J J V T V N R U Q S C U T T H R O A T T R O U T Q T K V
E S L E S Y J M T U W R I E M O T T E R U E X G N V J S
A F T T Q G C A N A D A G O O S E A P W J O C Q Q R N L
B L A C K B E A R M M H N B Z C O Y O T E N I Q A A V W
```

WORD LIST

GRIZZLY	PRONGHORN	RAVEN	MULE DEER	CUTTHROAT-
OTTER	BISON	CALLIOPE HUM-	BIGHORN SHEEP	TROUT
MOUNTAIN LION	BEAVER	MINGBIRD	MARMOT	COYOTE
ELK	TRUMPETER SWAN	BLACK BEAR	WHITE PELICAN	
MOOSE	CANADA GOOSE	WOLF	MAGPIE	

39

Crossword Puzzle: Park Facts

Across:

1. Stone copy of a tree
3. The name of the park's loop road and a geyser
4. Yellowstone & surrounding areas are managed as the Greater Yellowstone _____.

9. Some lava flows cooled to form _____ columns.
10. First white man to travel through Yellowstone
13. The Native American tribe that lived in Yellowstone year round
14. Wooden trail that protects people and resources

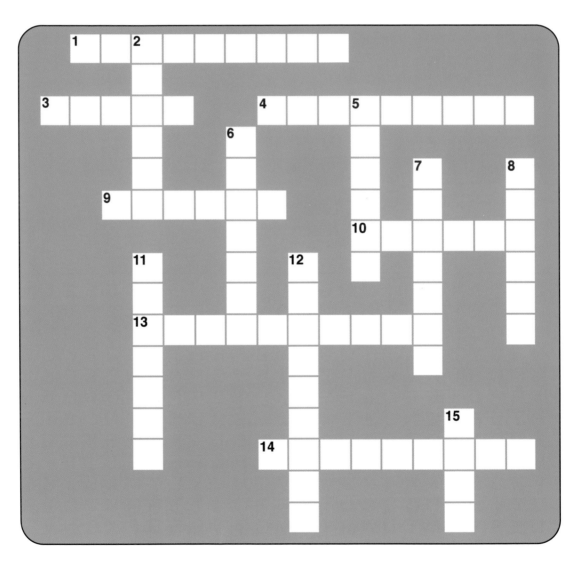

Answers: page 44

Down:

2. A type of plant community found on high mountains. Alpine _____
5. This tree has sharp, square needles.
6. This gas makes some thermal features smell rotten. Hydrogen _____

7. A giant volcanic basin within Yellowstone
8. Another name for a whistlepig
11. A favorite recreational activity is fly _____.
12. World's tallest active geyser
15. The longest wood hotel in the world

Nature Notes

Explorer's Checklist: Keep track of your discoveries. Your notes will help you remember your visit. If you come back to the park, your notes might help you refind a special place.

Geysers	Date	Duration	Height	Observations
☐ Anemone [15]				
☐ Beehive [15]				
☐ Castle [15]				
☐ Clepsydra [20]				
☐ Cliff [16]				
☐ Daisy [15]				
☐ Echinus [22]				
☐ Giant [15]				
☐ Grand [15]				
☐ Great Fountain [19]				
☐ Grotto [15]				
☐ Lone Star [14]				
☐ Old Faithful [15]				
☐ Plume [15]				
☐ Riverside [15]				
☐ Steamboat [22]				
☐ White Dome [19]				
☐ _____				
☐ _____				

Thermal Features	Date	Observations
☐ Crested Pool [15]		
☐ Emerald Pool [16]		
☐ fumarole		
☐ Grand Prismatic [18]		
☐ Minerva Terrace [1]		
☐ Morning Glory [15]		
☐ mud pot		
☐ Sapphire Pool [17]		
☐ _____		

Animals:	Date	Location	Observations
☐ bald eagle			
☐ bighorn sheep			
☐ bison			
☐ black bear			
☐ Canada goose			
☐ chipmunk			
☐ coyote			
☐ cutthroat trout			
☐ elk			
☐ grizzly			
☐ ground squirrel			
☐ marmot			
☐ moose			
☐ mule deer			
☐ osprey			
☐ otter			
☐ pronghorn			
☐ raven			
☐ trumpeter swan			
☐ white pelican			
☐ wolf			
☐ _____			
☐ _____			

Fun Things I Did:	Where	The best part about this was:
☐ took a hike		
☐ camped		
☐ took a boat ride		
☐ drove Grand Loop		
☐ went to a ranger program		
☐ visited an historic site		
☐ went fishing		
☐ took a stagecoach ride		
☐ watched wildlife		

Places to Visit:	When	The best part about this was...
☐ Biscuit Basin	_____	_____
☐ Black Sand Basin	_____	_____
☐ Continental Divide	_____	_____
☐ Dunraven Pass	_____	_____
☐ Firehole Lake Drive	_____	_____
☐ Fishing Bridge	_____	_____
☐ Fountain Paint Pots	_____	_____
☐ Grand Canyon	_____	_____
☐ Grant Visitor Center	_____	_____
☐ Madison	_____	_____
☐ Mammoth Hot Springs	_____	_____
☐ Midway Geyser Basin	_____	_____
☐ Mount Washburn	_____	_____
☐ Mud Volcano	_____	_____
☐ Norris Geyser Basin	_____	_____
☐ Obsidian Cliff	_____	_____
☐ Old Faithful	_____	_____
☐ Petrified Tree	_____	_____
☐ Ranger Museum	_____	_____
☐ Sheepeater Cliff	_____	_____
☐ Tower Fall	_____	_____
☐ Upper Geyser Basin	_____	_____
☐ West Thumb	_____	_____
☐ _____	_____	_____
☐ _____	_____	_____

Ask a Ranger: Write down any questions you think of while exploring the park. Next time you see a ranger, find out the answer and record it here in your notes.

_____

_____

_____

_____

_____

_____

_____

Answer Page

Fact Or Fiction: Explorer Thermometer

How many "Fact or Fiction" questions did you get right on your first guess? Compare your results with the Explorer Thermometer below. Which kind of Explorer are you?

Correct Answers

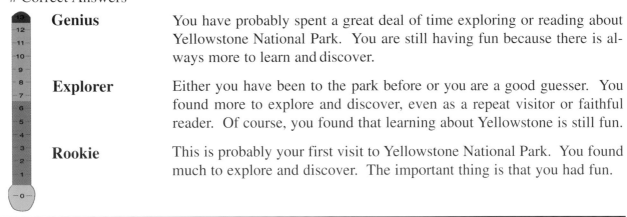

Genius   You have probably spent a great deal of time exploring or reading about Yellowstone National Park. You are still having fun because there is always more to learn and discover.

Explorer   Either you have been to the park before or you are a good guesser. You found more to explore and discover, even as a repeat visitor or faithful reader. Of course, you found that learning about Yellowstone is still fun.

Rookie   This is probably your first visit to Yellowstone National Park. You found much to explore and discover. The important thing is that you had fun.

Mini Mystery *(page 32)*: 1). The two new stories that Jim Bridger told were tall tales. 2). The stories that Tom related were true. 3). The fountain that spouts every hour is Old Faithful Geyser (page 6). The fountain that warms the river water is Riverside Geyser (page 9). The boiling mud could be Fountain Paint Pots or Mud Volcano (page 11). 4. The glass mountain is Obsidian Cliff (page 16). It is not really clear nor is it like a telescope. Obsidian is a black glassy rock. Today, lichen covers much of the cliff's glassy surface. 5. The only truth to the peetrified story was the petrified trees (page 17).

Word Search Clues *(page 39)*

1. elk
2. grizzly
3. moose
4. pronghorn
5. bison
6. trumpeter swan
7. Canada goose

Crossword Puzzle   *(page 40)*

Across

1. petrified
3. Grand
4. ecosystem
9. basalt
10. Colter
13. Sheepeater
14. boardwalk

Down

2. tundra
5. spruce
6. sulfide
7. caldera
8. marmot
11. fishing
12. Steamboat
15. Lake

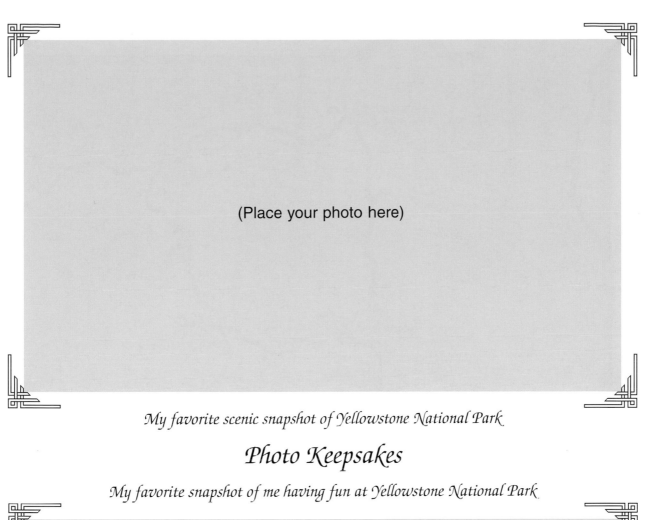

(Place your photo here)

My favorite scenic snapshot of Yellowstone National Park

Photo Keepsakes

My favorite snapshot of me having fun at Yellowstone National Park

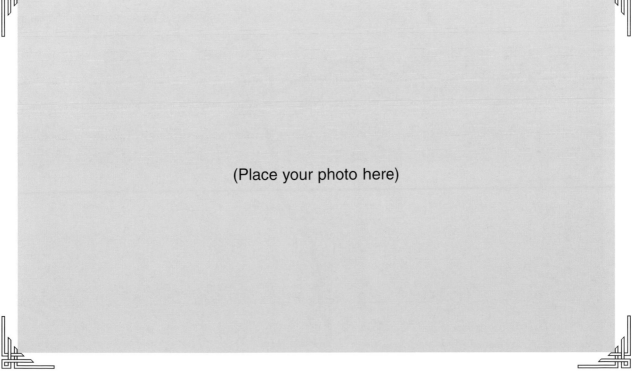

(Place your photo here)

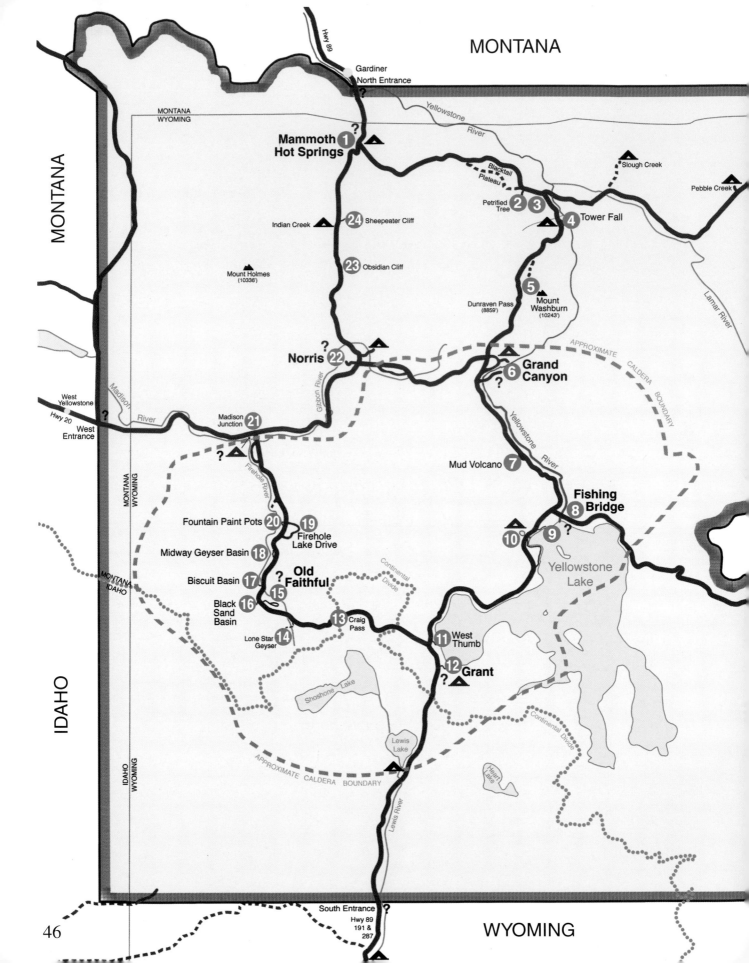

MONTANA

Hwy 89

Gardiner
North Entrance

?

MONTANA
WYOMING

Yellowstone River

Slough Creek

Pebble Creek

MONTANA

**Mammoth
Hot Springs** 1

?

Blacktail
Plateau

Petrified
Tree

2 3

4 **Tower Fall**

Indian Creek 24 Sheepeater Cliff

Lamar River

23 Obsidian Cliff

Mount Holmes
(10336')

5

Mount
Washburn
(10243')

Dunraven Pass
(8859')

APPROXIMATE CALDERA

Norris 22 ?

6 **Grand
Canyon**

?

BOUNDARY

West
Yellowstone

Hwy 20

West
Entrance

?

Madison River

Gibbon River

Madison
Junction 21

?

Firehole River

Mud Volcano 7

Yellowstone River

**Fishing
Bridge** 8

9 ?

MONTANA
WYOMING

Fountain Paint Pots 20 19 Firehole
Lake Drive

Midway Geyser Basin 18

Continental
Divide

Biscuit Basin 17 ? **Old
Faithful**

MONTANA
IDAHO

Black
Sand
Basin 16

15

Lone Star
Geyser 14

13 Craig
Pass

10

**Yellowstone
Lake**

11 **West
Thumb**

12 **Grant**
?

Shoshone Lake

Continental Divide

IDAHO

IDAHO
WYOMING

Lewis Lake

Heart
Lake

APPROXIMATE CALDERA BOUNDARY

Lewis River

South Entrance ?

Hwy 89
191 &
287

WYOMING

YELLOWSTONE NATIONAL PARK

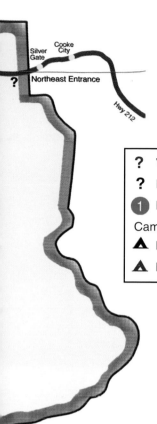

Points of Interest

1. Mammoth Hot Springs
2. Petrified Tree
3. Roosevelt Lodge
4. Tower Fall
5. Mount Washburn/ Dunraven Pass
6. Grand Canyon of Yellowstone
7. Mud Volcano
8. Fishing Bridge
9. Lake Village
10. Bridge Bay
11. West Thumb Geyser Basin
12. Grant Village
13. Craig Pass
14. Lone Star Geyser
15. Old Faithful/ Upper Geyser Basin
16. Black Sand Basin
17. Biscuit Basin
18. Midway Geyser Basin
19. Firehole Lake Drive
20. Fountain Paint Pots
21. Madison Junction
22. Norris Geyser Basin
23. Obsidian Cliff
24. Sheepeater Cliff

Legend:

- **?** Visitor Center
- **?** Information
- **1** Point of Interest

Campgrounds:
- ▲ First-Come
- ▲ Reservable

Mileage Chart

Direction of Travel:
- Clockwise
- Counterclockwise
- Via Norris/Canyon Road

From: \ To:	Canyon	Fishing Bridge / Lake Village	Madison	Mammoth	Norris	Old Faithful	Roosevelt / Tower Junction	West Thumb / Grant Village
Canyon		16	26	33/37	12	42/54	19	37
Fishing Bridge / Lake Village	16		42/54	49/53	28/68	38/58	35	21
Madison	26	42/54		35	14	16	45/53	33
Mammoth	33/37	53/49	35		21	51	18	68/74
Norris	12	28/68	14	21		30	31/39	47/49
Old Faithful	42/54	38/58	16	51	30		61	17
Roosevelt / Tower Junction	19	35	45/53	18	31/39	61		56
West Thumb / Grant	37	21	33	68/74	47/49	17	56	
East Entrance	43	27	69/81	76/116	55/95	65/85	62	48/102
North Entrance	38/42	58/94	40	5	26	56	23	73/79
Northeast Entrance	48	64	74/82	47	60/68	90/102	29	85/115
South Entrance	59/81	43/97	55	90/96	69/71	39	78/108	22
West Entrance	40	56/68	14	49	28	30	59/67	47

Loop Mileages: Grand Loop— 142 miles; Lower Loop— 96 miles; Upper Loop— 70 miles

Glossary: What Does That Word Mean?

acid - a sour chemical. A strong acid can dissolve some substances.

algae - a large group of plant-like organisms that do not have roots or flowers. They are mainly found in water. **alga** - a single algae organism.

bacteria - very tiny organisms that are neither plants nor animals. **bacterium** - a single bacteria organism.

basalt - a hard, dense, dark volcanic rock.

basin - a large, bowl-shaped depression in the surface of the land.

bill - a suggested law.

caldera - a large crater or basin formed by volcanic explosion or collapse of a volcanic cone.

carrion - dead and decaying animals.

concessions - a business which has a government permit to provide a public service.

enzyme - a protein produced by living organisms. It's used to start a biochemical process.

erode - to slowly wear or wash away.

erosion - the process of slowly washing or wearing away the earth's surface.

eruption - a sudden action which releases or forces something out.

expedition - a journey made for a specific reason. Often it is a journey to explore a certain area.

extinction - when something no longer exists.

geyser - a hot spring that intermittently spouts a column of water and steam into the air.

hibernation - to be in a very long deep sleep.

habitat - place where wild animals and plants live and grow. It includes the food, water, space and shelter that they need.

hydrothermal - something that uses hot water.

lava - hot liquid rock that reaches the earth's surface through a volcano or crack.

magma - hot liquid rock material under the earth's crust.

migrate - to change location periodically, especially by moving seasonally from one region to another.

mineral - a substance found in nature that is not an animal or plant. example: salt, gold.

natural resources - natural materials that are valuable to people. examples: timber, water, minerals.

petrified - wood or other organic matter that has been changed into a stone replica.

plateau - an area of flat land that is raised above the surrounding country.

threatened - to be in danger of disappearing or becoming extinct.

thermal - something related to or caused by heat.

thermal features - a natural formation that is created or affected by heat.

Index